Facts About the Killer Whale

By Lisa Strattin

© 2019 Lisa Strattin

FREE BOOK

FREE FOR ALL SUBSCRIBERS

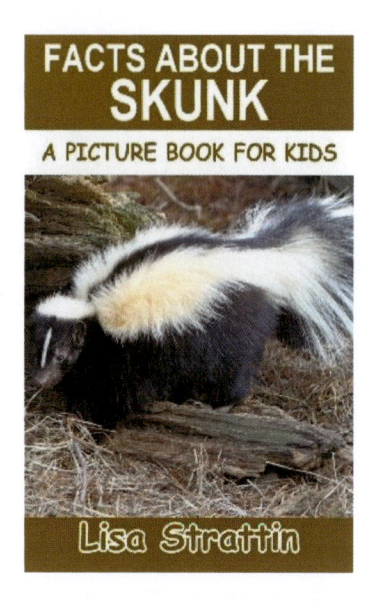

LisaStrattin.com/Subscribe-Here

BOX SET

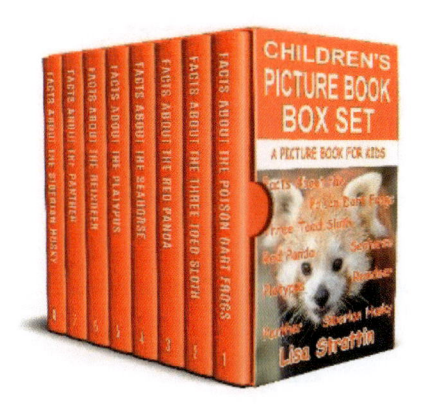

- FACTS ABOUT THE POISON DART FROGS
- FACTS ABOUT THE THREE TOED SLOTH
  - FACTS ABOUT THE RED PANDA
  - FACTS ABOUT THE SEAHORSE
  - FACTS ABOUT THE PLATYPUS
  - FACTS ABOUT THE REINDEER
  - FACTS ABOUT THE PANTHER
- FACTS ABOUT THE SIBERIAN HUSKY

LisaStrattin.com/BookBundle

Facts for Kids Picture Books by Lisa Strattin

Little Blue Penguin, Vol 92

Chipmunk, Vol 5

Frilled Lizard, Vol 39

Blue and Gold Macaw, Vol 13

Poison Dart Frogs, Vol 50

Blue Tarantula, Vol 115

African Elephants, Vol 8

Amur Leopard, Vol 89

Sabre Tooth Tiger, Vol 167

Baboon, Vol 174

Sign Up for New Release Emails Here

LisaStrattin.com/subscribe-here

All rights reserved. No part of this book may be reproduced by any means whatsoever without the written permission from the author, except brief portions quoted for purpose of review.

All information in this book has been carefully researched and checked for factual accuracy. However, the author and publisher makes no warranty, express or implied, that the information contained herein is appropriate for every individual, situation or purpose and assume no responsibility for errors or omissions. The reader assumes the risk and full responsibility for all actions, and the author will not be held responsible for any loss or damage, whether consequential, incidental, special or otherwise, that may result from the information presented in this book.

All images are free for use or purchased from stock photo sites or royalty free for commercial use.

Some coloring pages might be of the general species due to lack of available images.

I have relied on my own observations as well as many different sources for this book and I have done my best to check facts and give credit where it is due. In the event that any material is used without proper permission, please contact me so that the oversight can be corrected.

COVER IMAGE

By Robert Pittman - NOAA (http://www.afsc.noaa.gov/Quarterly/amj2005/divrptsNMML3.htm]), Public Domain, https://commons.wikimedia.org/w/index.php?curid=1433661

ADDITIONAL IMAGES

https://www.flickr.com/photos/37195641@N03/8049964362/

https://www.flickr.com/photos/livenature/2190700451/

https://www.flickr.com/photos/spencer77/4774659226/

https://www.flickr.com/photos/archer10/36407218133/

https://www.flickr.com/photos/archer10/37049851652/

https://www.flickr.com/photos/cmichel67/40304080015/

https://www.flickr.com/photos/35142635@N05/7459706002/

https://www.flickr.com/photos/rojer/4884823771/

https://www.flickr.com/photos/mikebaird/13962163948/

https://www.flickr.com/photos/ojoswis_snaps/6203322213/

TABLE OF CONTENTS

INTRODUCTION 9

CHARACTERISTICS 11

APPEARANCE 13

VOCALIZATIONS 15

LIFE SPAN 17

SIZE 19

REPRODUCTION 21

DIET 23

ENEMIES 25

SUITABILITY AS PETS 27

INTRODUCTION

Killer Whales (Orca) are found in all of the world's oceans, both hot and cold, from the freezing waters of the North and South Poles to very warm tropical seas.

The Killer Whale is the largest member of the dolphin family, and there are about 5 different species of them in the oceans.

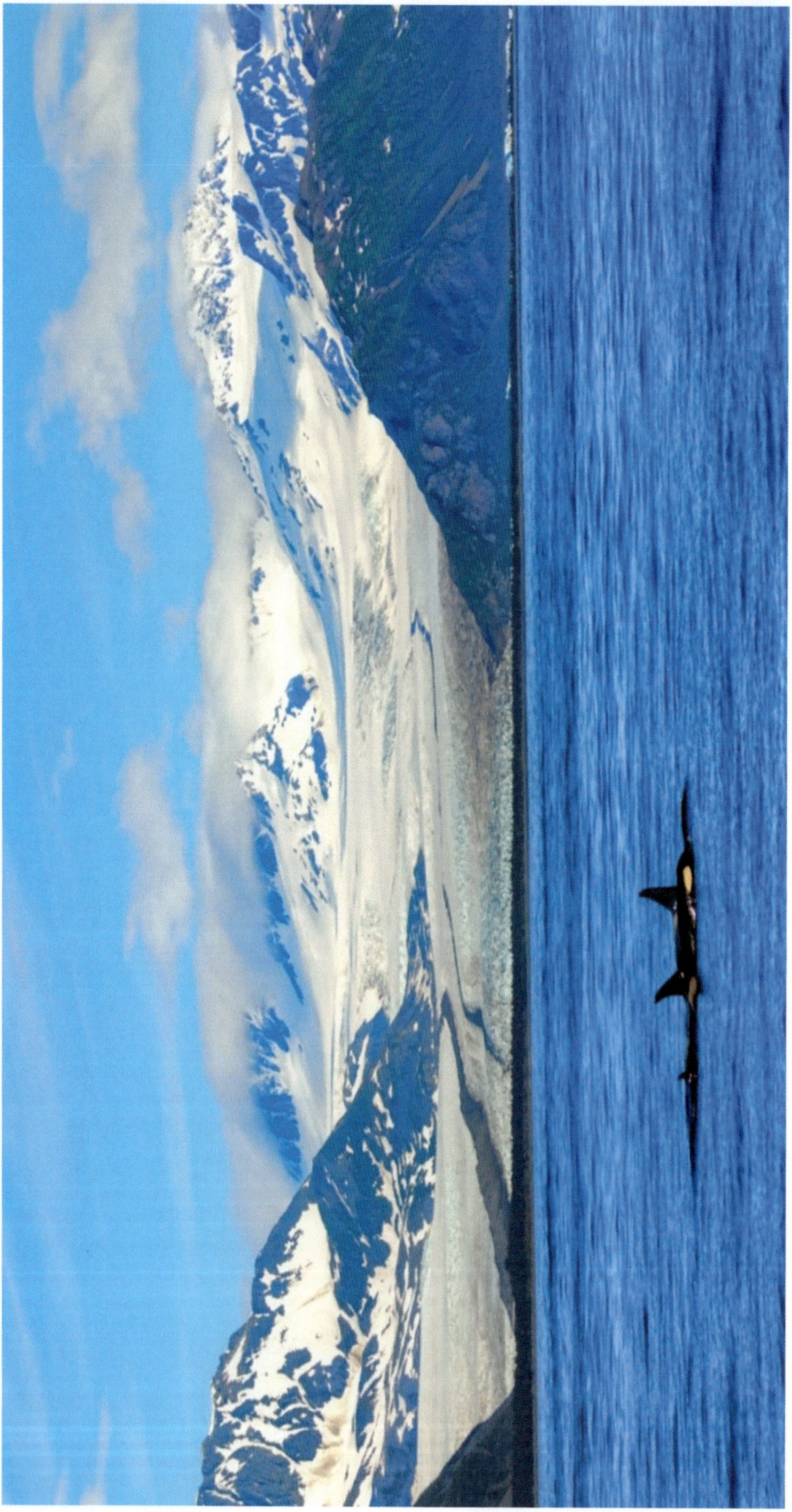

CHARACTERISTICS

The Killer Whale is a dominant hunter but gets their name from the huge amount of meat it eats, instead of an aggressive temperament. Some of them are known to be naturally acrobatic, although they are usually trained in zoos and aquariums.

They have a top speed of around 30 miles an hour but can travel at around 25 miles per hour for long periods of time. It is common for them to swim more than 50 miles at this speed without stopping.

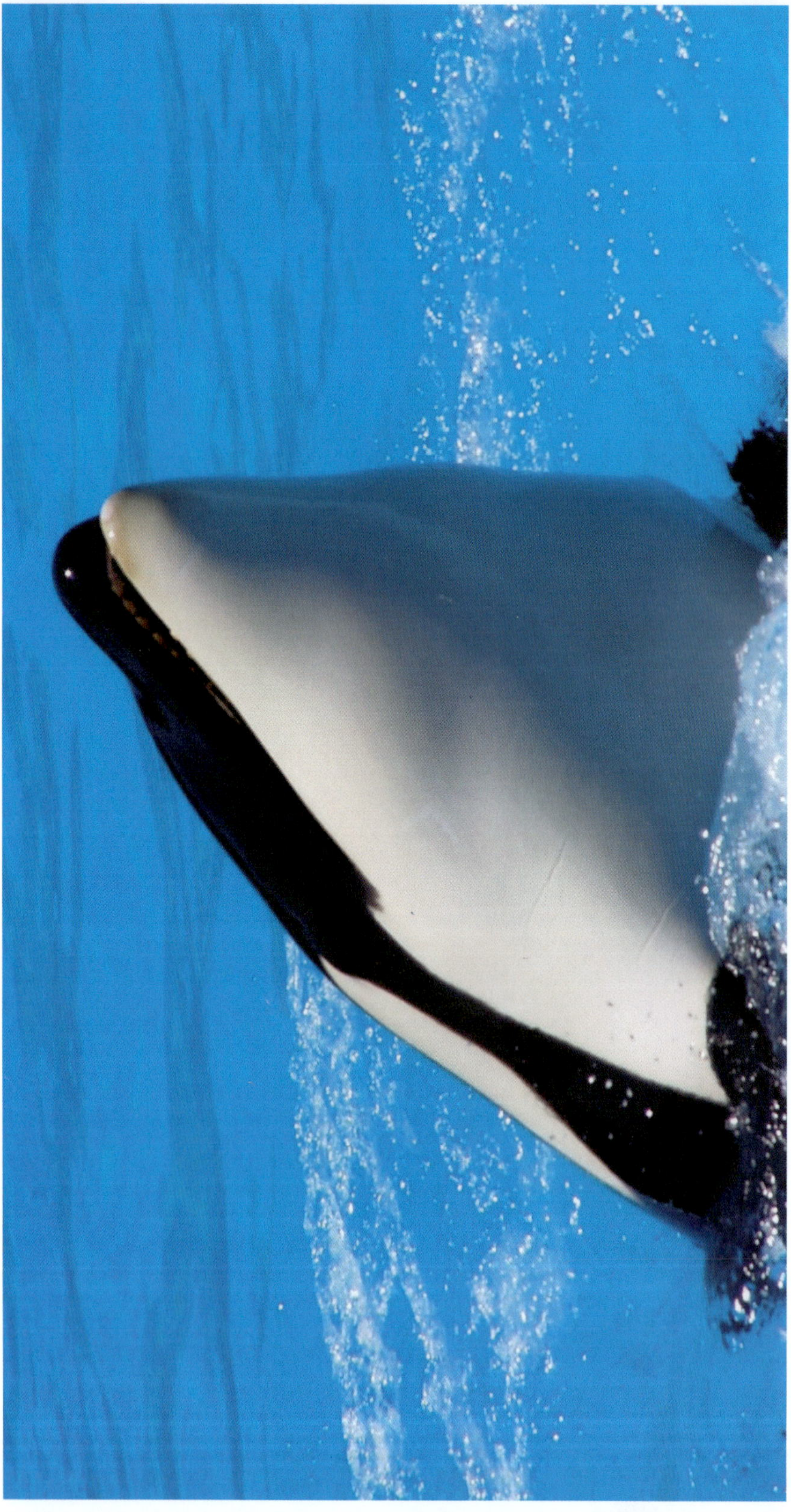

APPEARANCE

Killer Whales are large, stocky animals with a large dorsal fin. Their sharp black and white markings are the most distinctive feature.

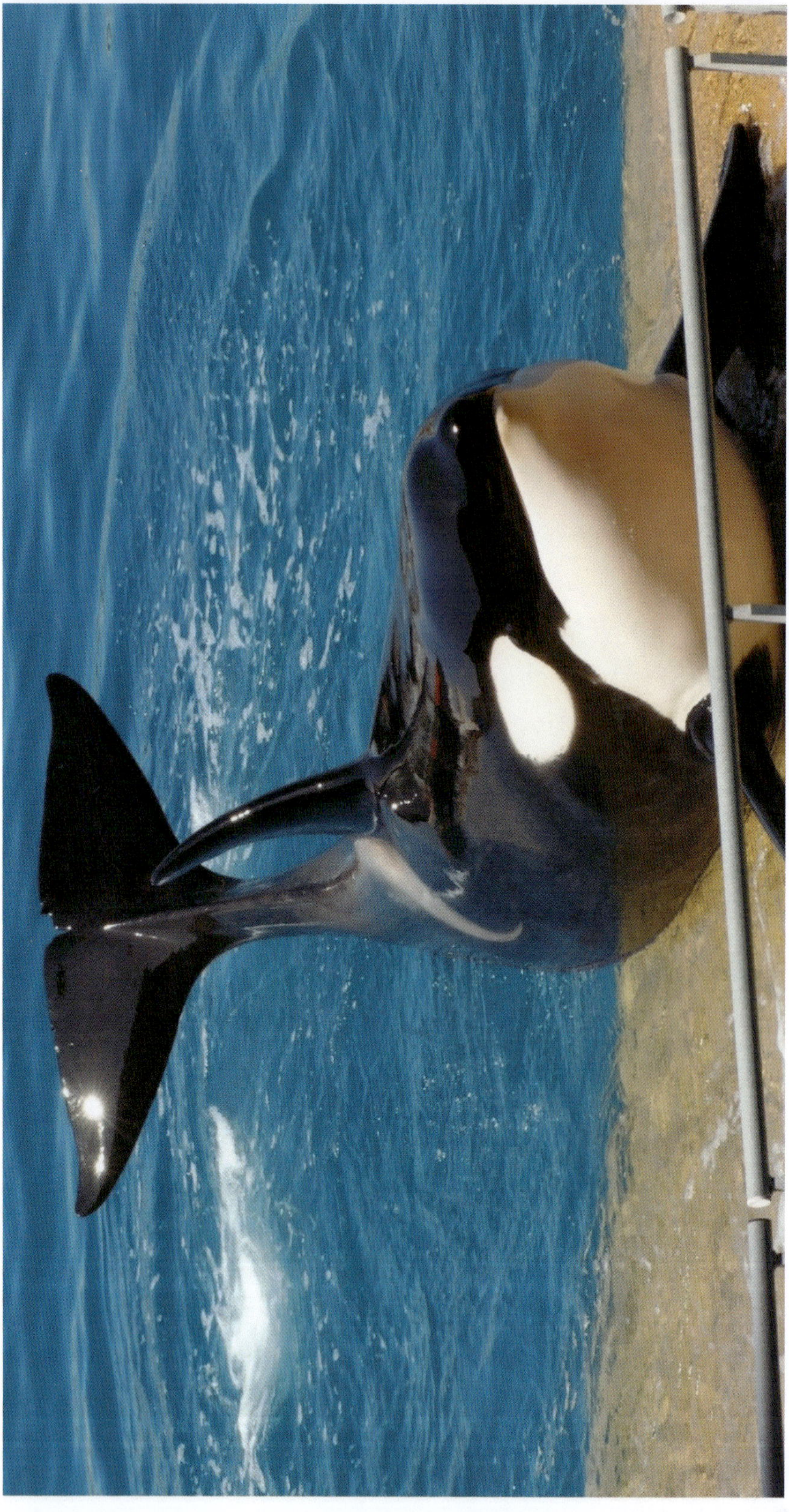

VOCALIZATIONS

As with their dolphin cousins, Killer Whales are extremely vocal animals and communicate between one another using clicks and whistles! This is called echolocation.

Killer Whales are known to at their most vocal and noisy when they are hunting. They are much calmer and quieter when they are resting.

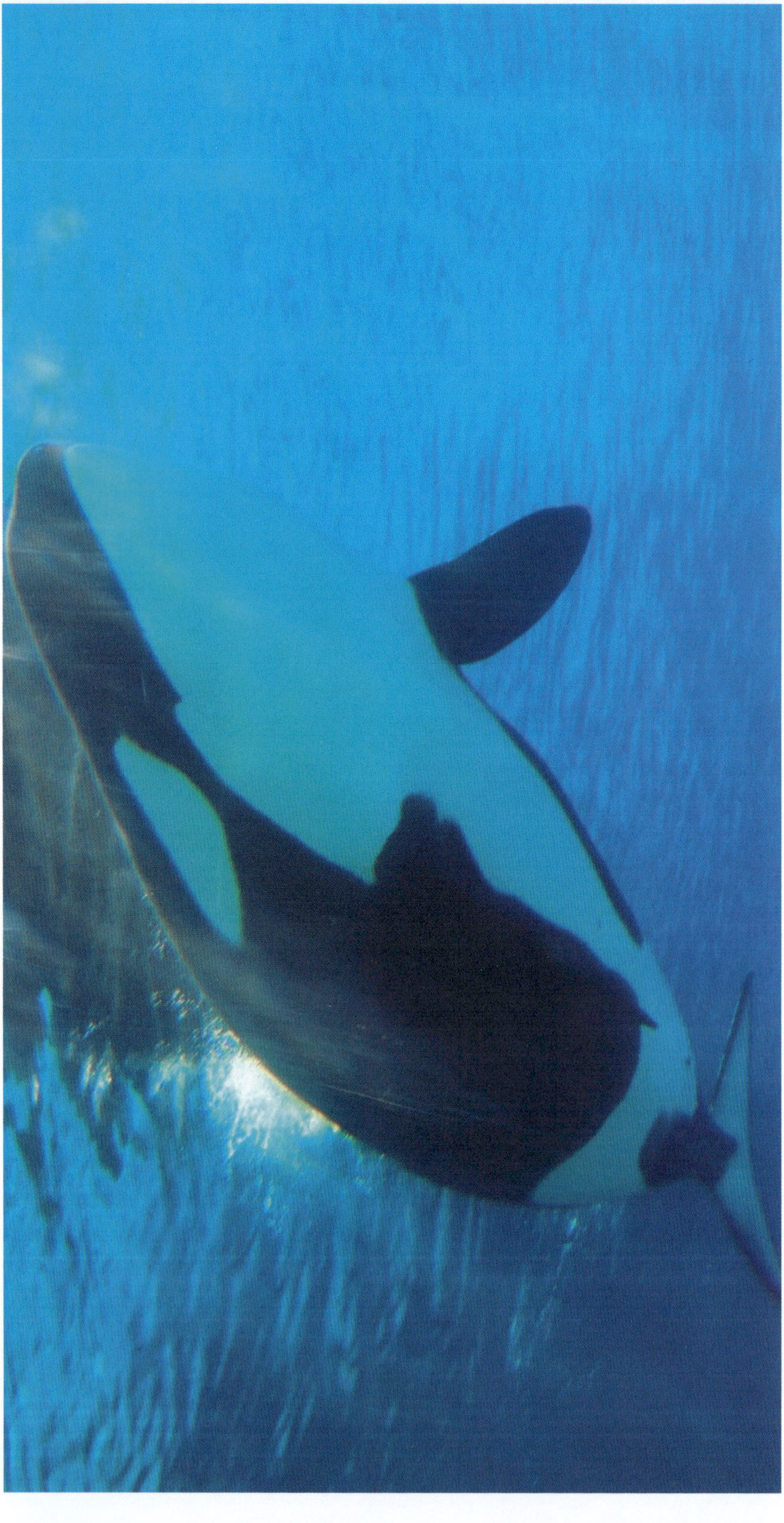

LIFE SPAN

Killer Whales can live until they are 60 years old. Interestingly, those that that are kept in captivity will often not live longer than 25 years, but in the wild they live for much longer.

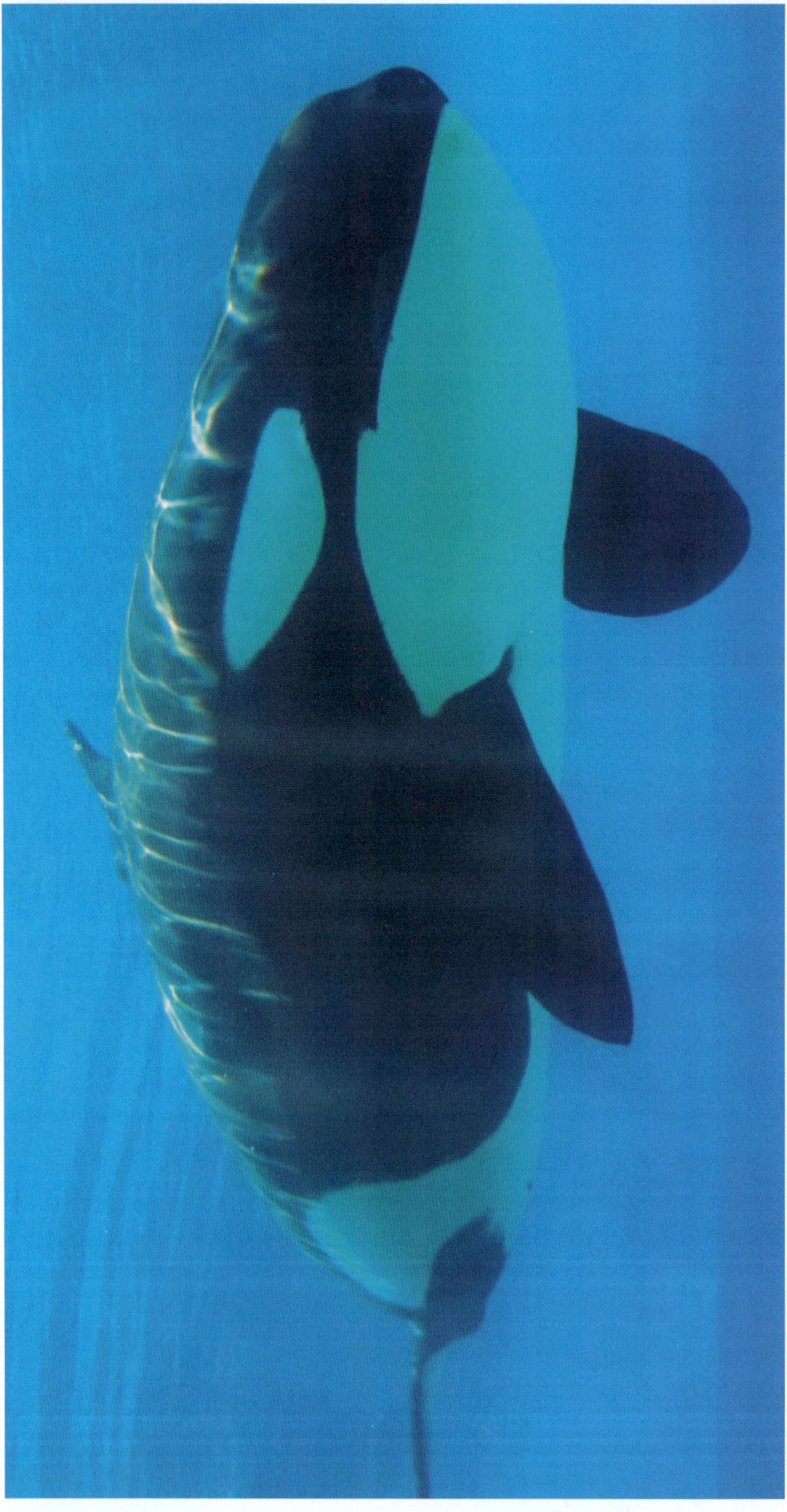

SIZE

Males are bigger than females, with males growing to around 25 feet in length. Females are slightly smaller, growing to around 23 feet in length.

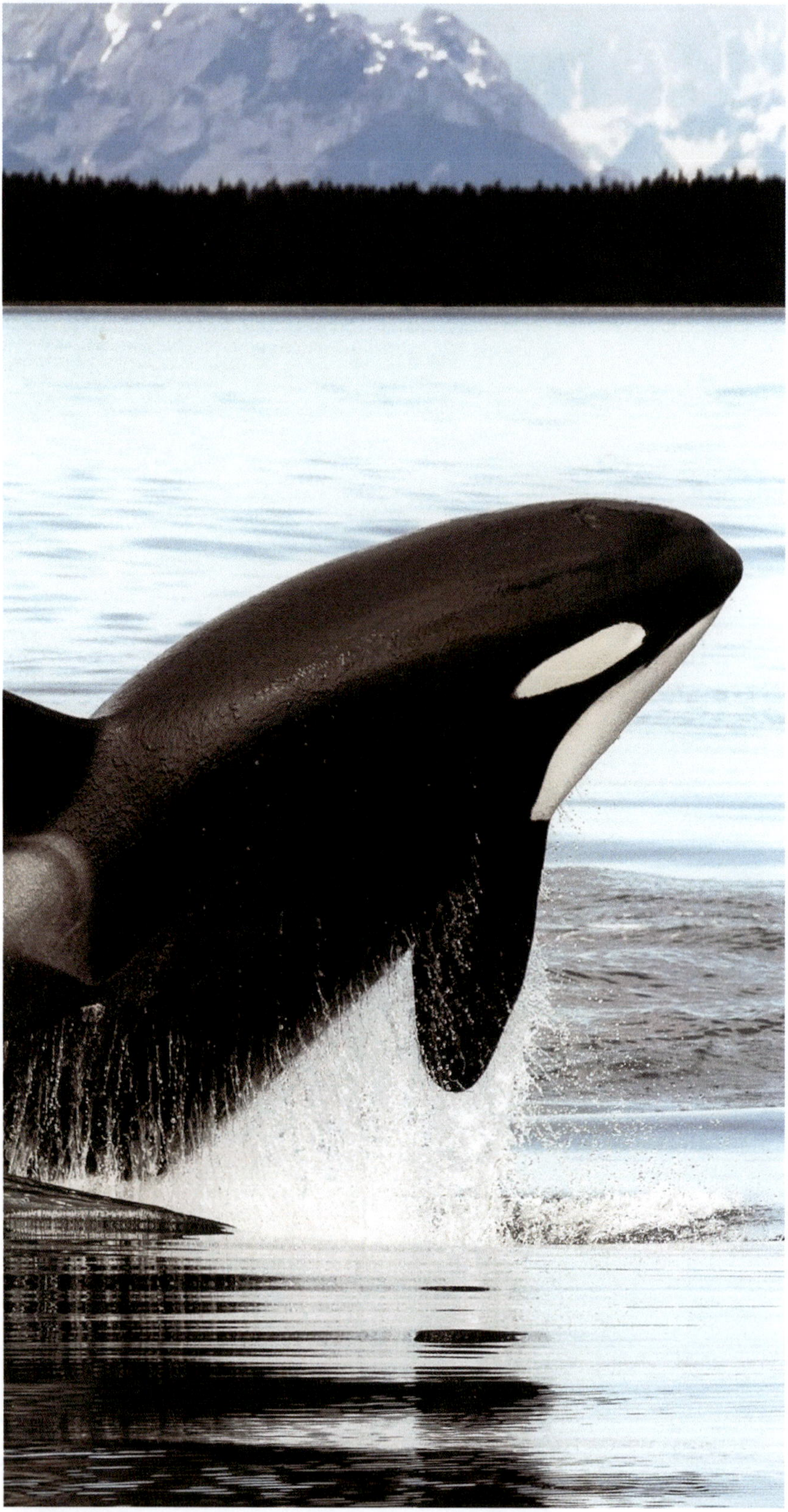

REPRODUCTION

Female Killer Whales give birth to one once every five years or so. Babies are born with a yellowish tint to the white parts of their skin, which fades into the brilliant white color as the baby matures. Mothers look after their calves (babies) for the first couple of years of life. Calves feed only on their mother's milk until they are about a year old, when they will begin to eat solid food.

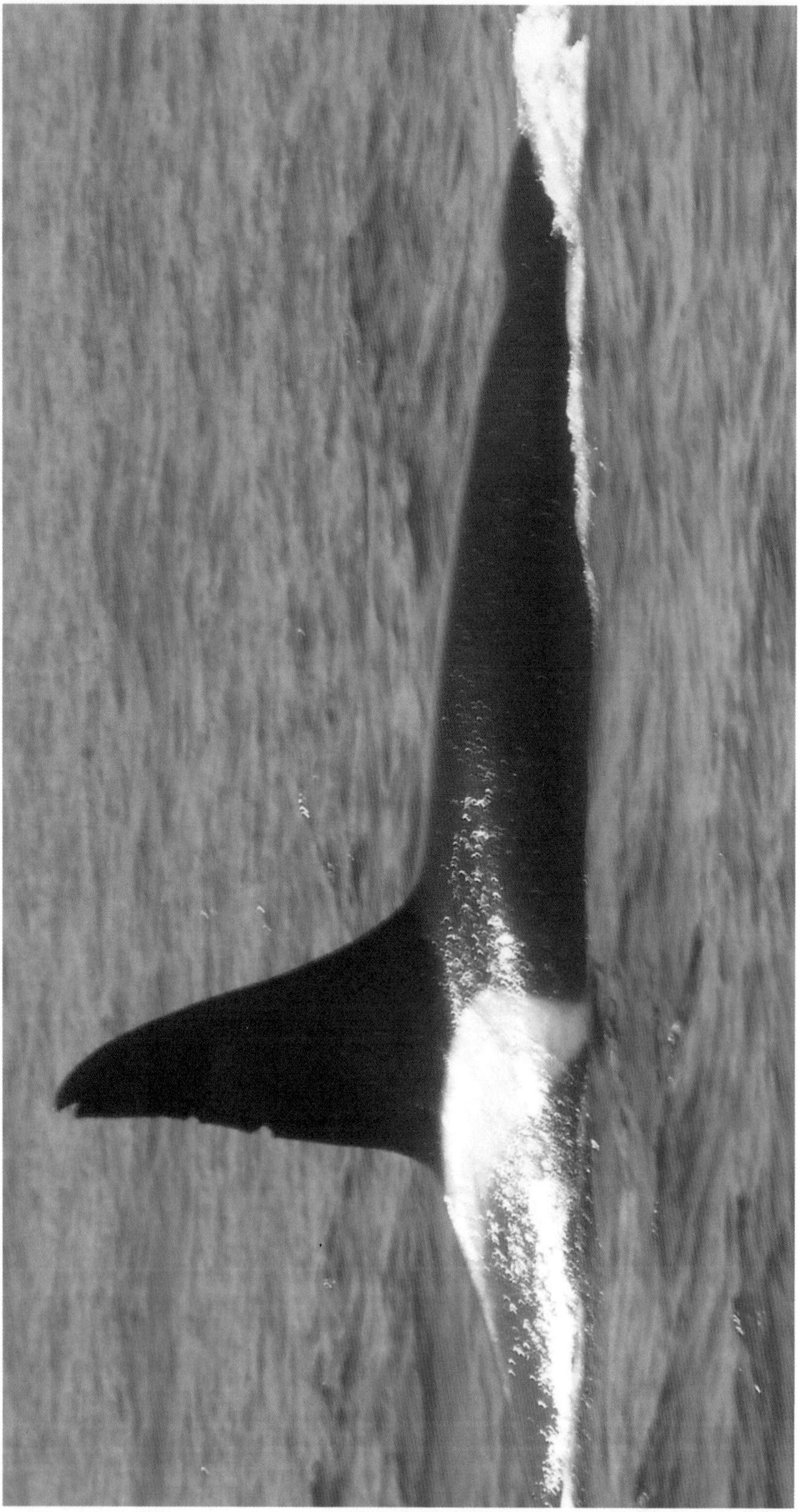

DIET

Killer Whales hunt in groups called pods that normally have from 6 to 40 members. They hunt larger fish, squid, octopuses, sea turtles, sharks, rays, seals and sea lions, as well as sea birds and mammals.

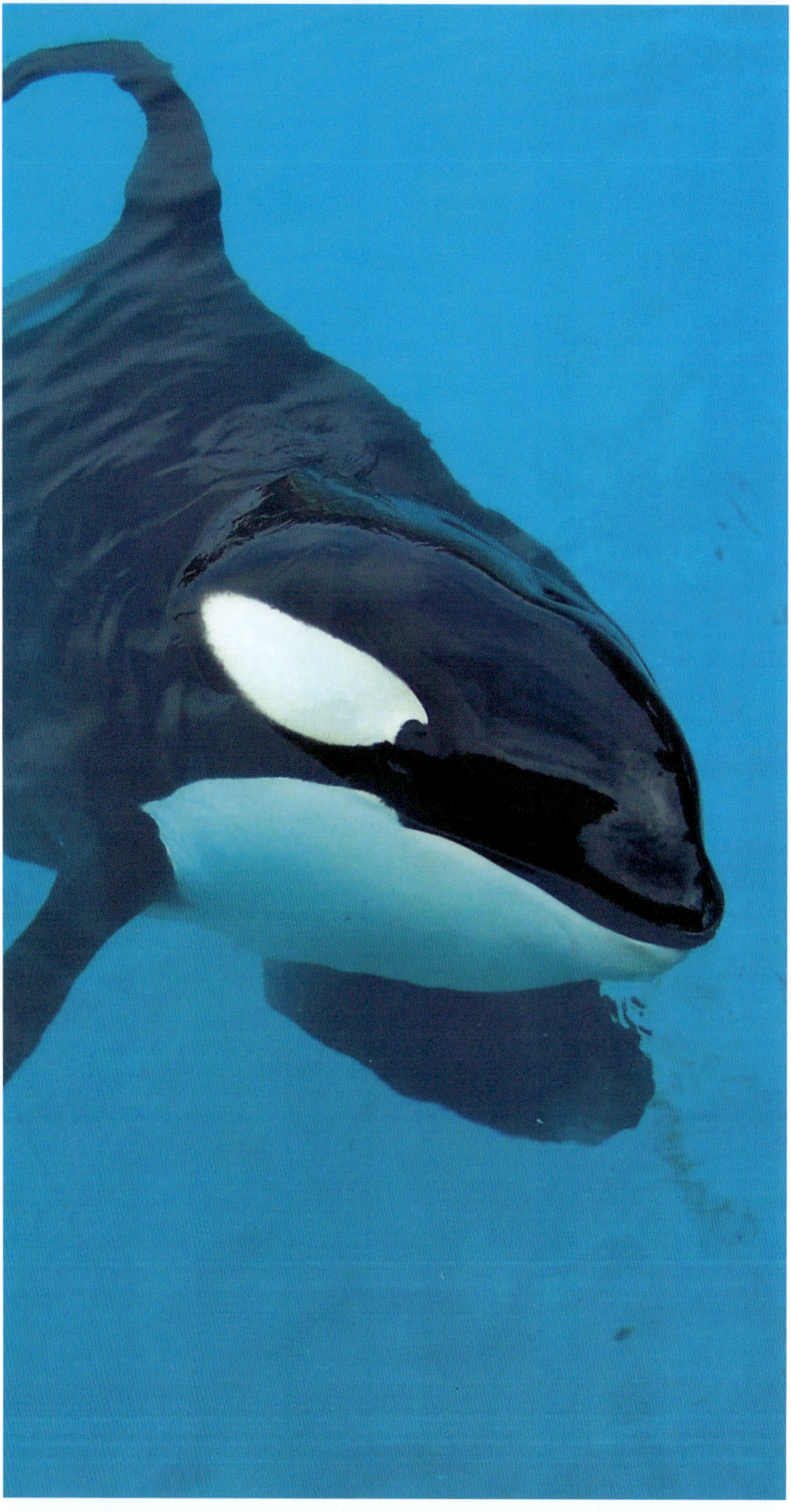

ENEMIES

Killer Whales are at the top of the food chain, no animal that is native to the ocean where they live hunts them.

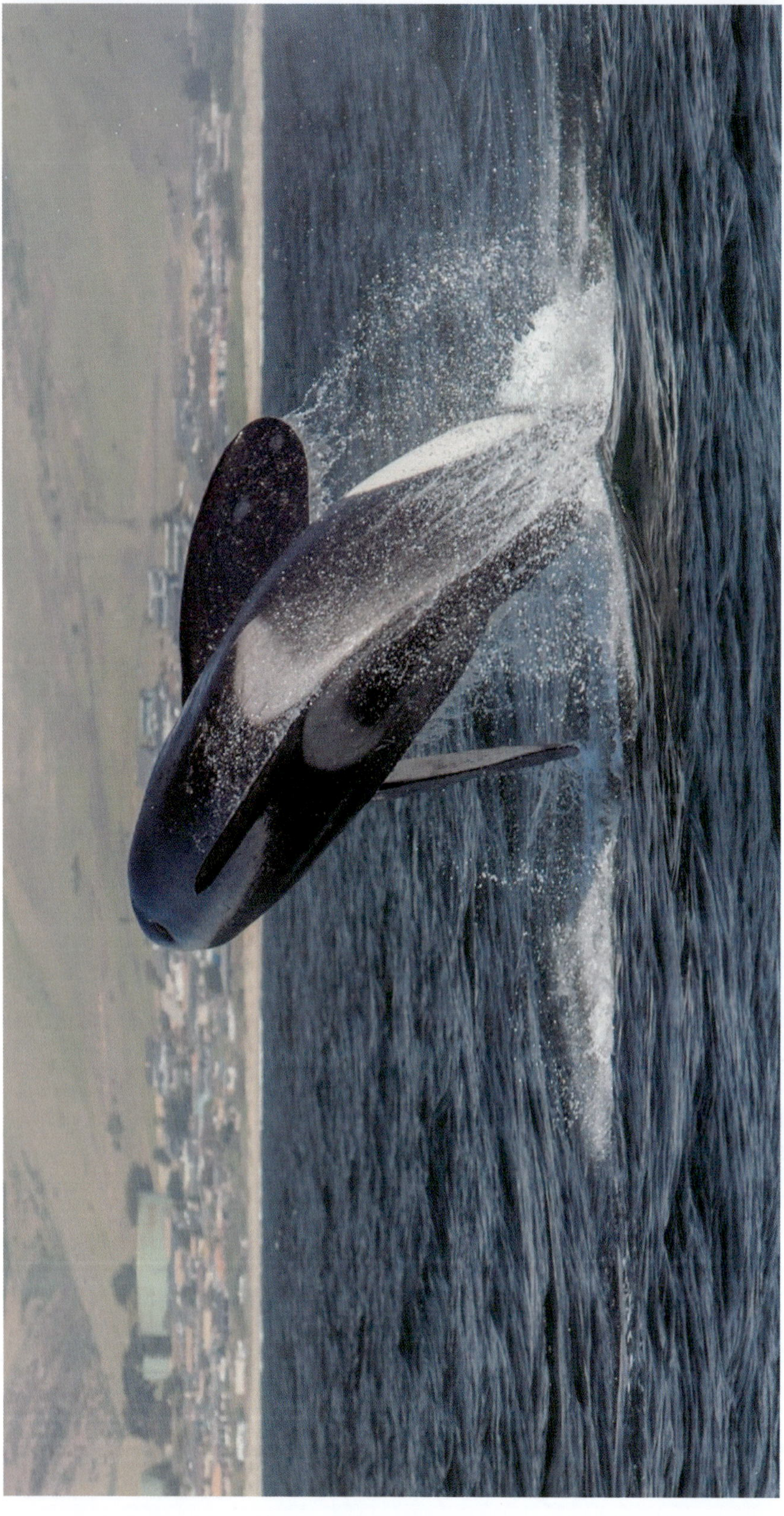

SUITABILITY AS PETS

Of course not. There is no way that you could have a Killer Whale as a house pet. However, there are many aquariums with suitable habitats for them where you can see them.

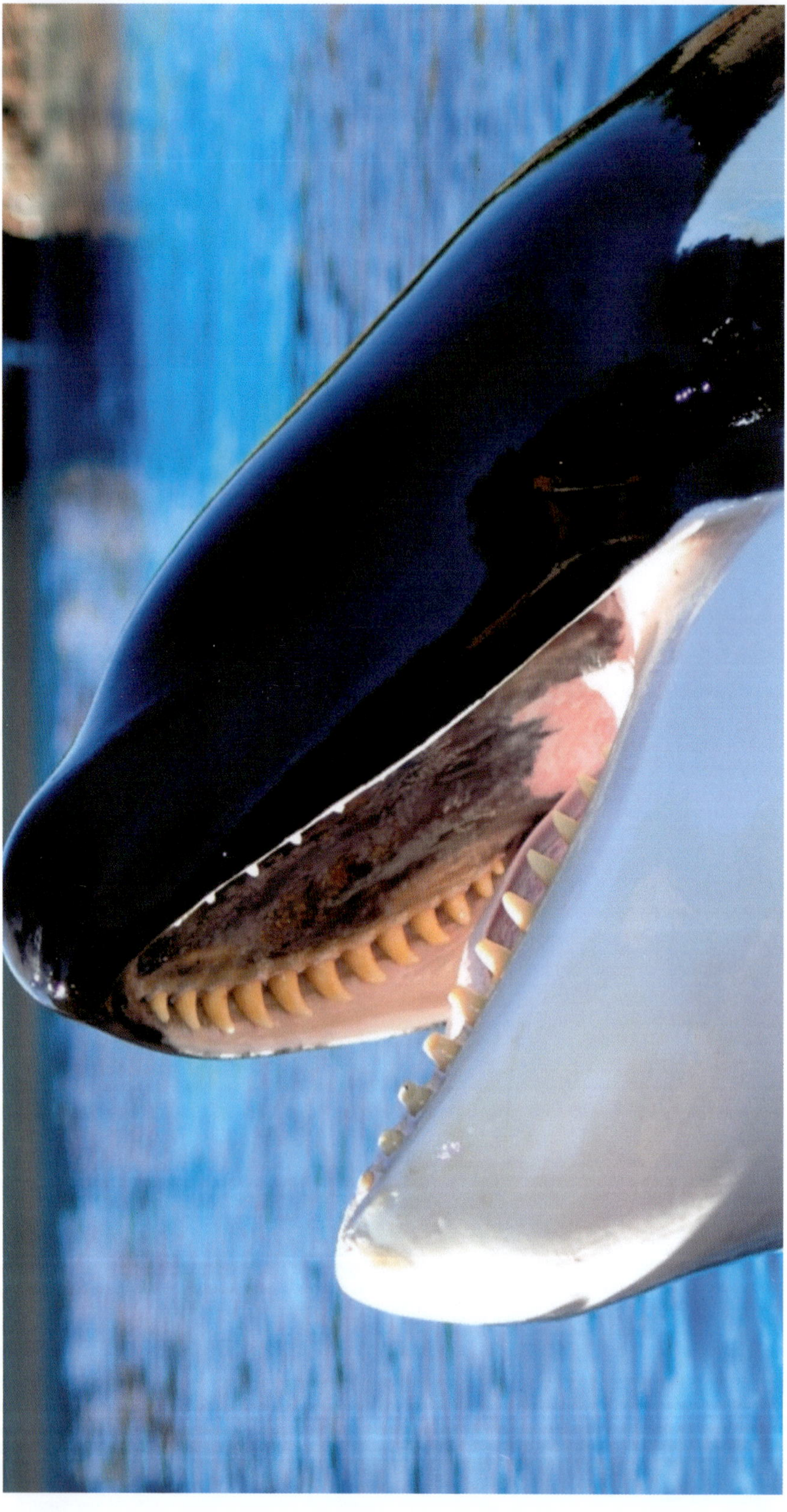

COLOR ME

COLOR ME

COLOR ME

COLOR ME

COLOR ME

COLOR ME

COLOR ME

COLOR ME

COLOR ME

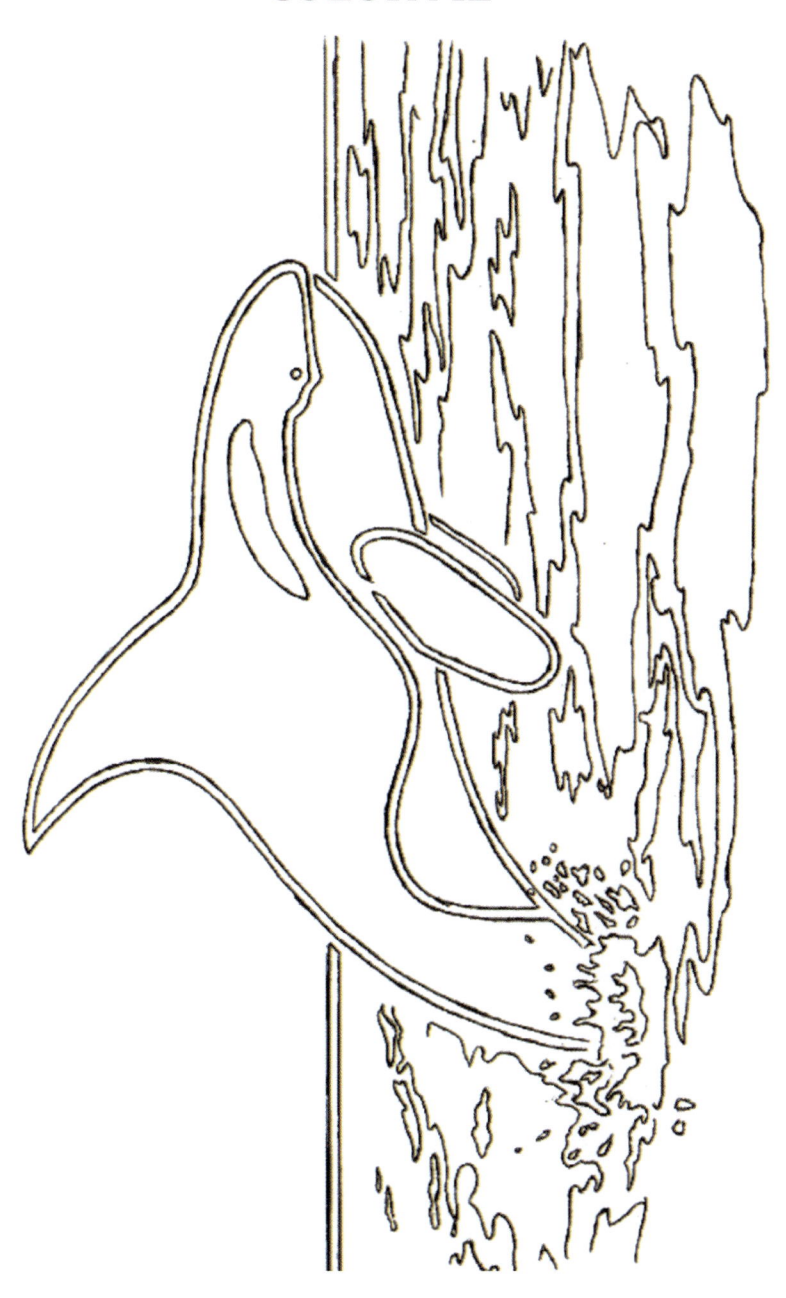

37

COLOR ME

Please leave me a review here:

LisaStrattin.com/Review-Vol-284

For more Kindle Downloads Visit Lisa Strattin Author Page on Amazon Author Central

amazon.com/author/lisastrattin

To see upcoming titles, visit my website at LisaStrattin.com– most books available on Kindle!

LisaStrattin.com

FREE BOOK

FOR ALL SUBSCRIBERS – SIGN UP NOW

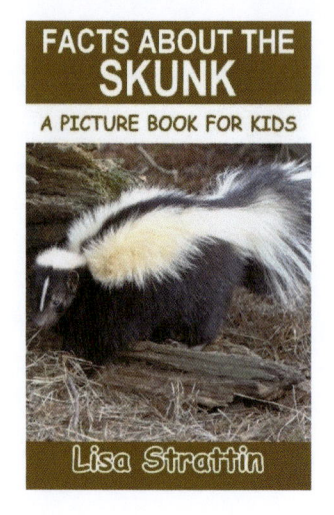

LisaStrattin.com/Subscribe-Here

LisaStrattin.com/Facebook

LisaStrattin.com/Youtube

Printed in Great Britain
by Amazon